THE GHOSTLY TALES OF DELAWARE

For my fun, spooky, wonderful family.
Thanks for all the awesome Halloween parties.

Published by Arcadia Children's Books
A Division of Arcadia Publishing
Charleston, SC
www.arcadiapublishing.com

First published 2023

Manufactured in the United States

ISBN 978-1-4671-9738-0

Library of Congress Control Number: 2023937852

Images used courtesy of Shutterstock.com; p. 8 Smallbones/Public domain/Wikimedia Commons; p. 58 : Joseph Sohm/Shutterstock.com; p. 86 Library of Congress, Prints & Photographs Division, HABS DEL,3-LAU.V,1-.

Spooky America

THE GHOSTLY TALES OF DELAWARE

CARIE JUETTNER

Adapted from *Haunted History of Delaware* by Josh Hitchens

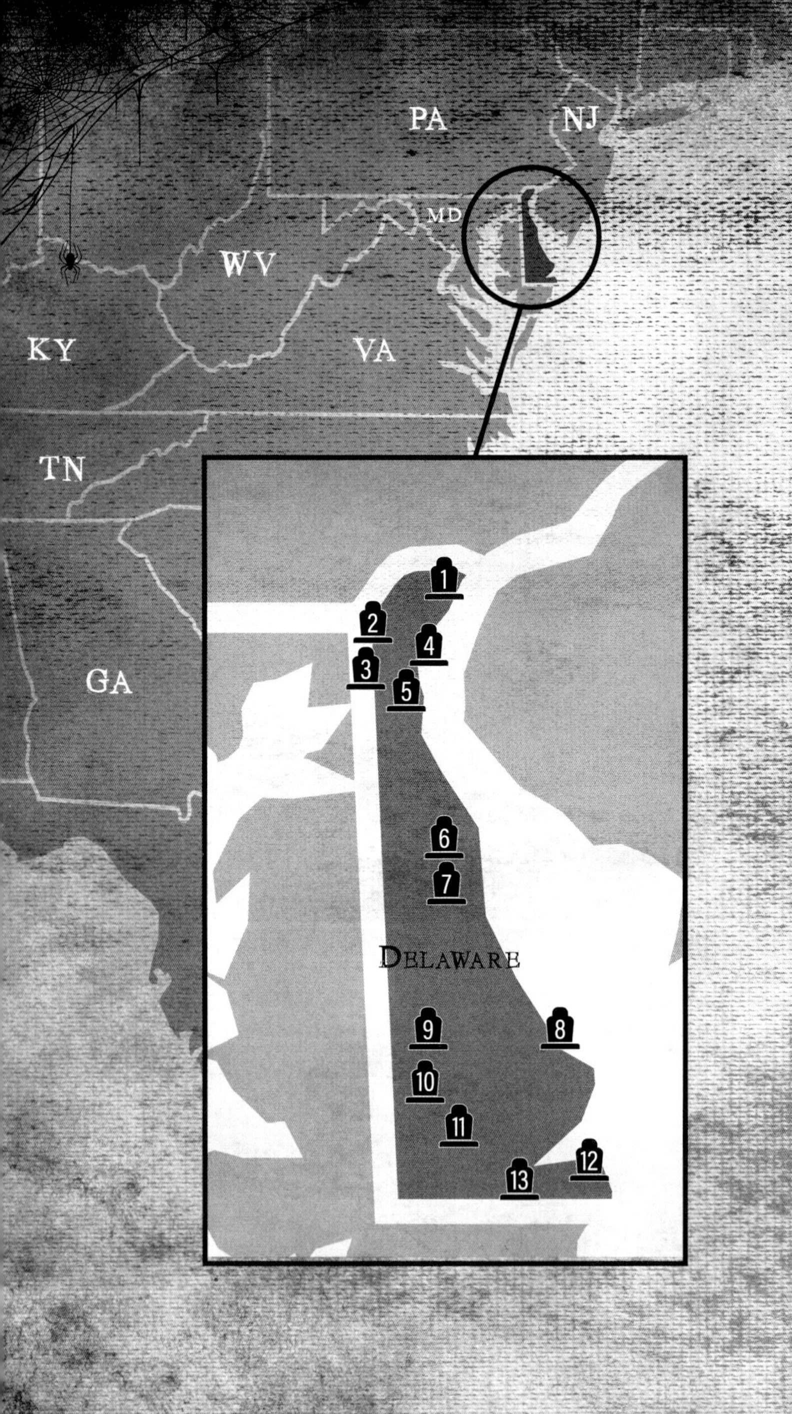

PA
NJ
MD
WV
KY
VA
TN
GA
Delaware
1
2
3
4
5
6
7
8
9
10
11
12
13

Table of Contents & Map Key

Let's Go on a Journey

It is nighttime, and you are traveling an unknown path. As your car enters a dark tunnel, you hear screams from somewhere in front of you. The car whips to the right, and suddenly you're face to face with a hideous ghoul! It swerves to the left, and a monster with glowing eyes reaches for you! Within moments, ghosts are popping up everywhere you look. Heart pounding, you grip the armrests in both fear and delight, hoping this adventure is over soon and also never wanting it to end. You're on the famous Haunted Mansion ride at the Funland amusement park in Rehoboth Beach, Delaware.

Funland's phantoms might be fake, but a trip through Delaware is not as different from a trip through the Haunted Mansion as you might think. The state has plenty of real ghosts and witches and monsters. They're lurking in houses, behind trees, within graveyards, and beneath bridges, just waiting for you to wander by.

Delaware has a lot more to offer than just spooky sites. The state is filled with unique features, beautiful landscapes, and important American history. Delaware, which gets its name from Lord Thomas De La Warr, became the "First State" on December 7, 1787, beating Pennsylvania by just five days. Joe Biden, the 46th American president, is from Delaware. He owns homes in both Wilmington and Rehoboth Beach.

With an area of just under 2,500 square miles, Delaware is the second smallest state in the U.S., but what it lacks in size, it makes up for in charm. The state is packed full of historic landmarks and captivating museums, quiet country roads and bustling towns, scenic farmland and beautiful beaches. It's also filled with sinister stories and a past that sometimes refuses to stay buried.

Let's take a tour of Delaware, shall we? We'll check out the state's most haunted places, starting in the north at a *real* haunted mansion in

Wilmington, then stopping by Newark to meet a headless horseman before spending the night (if we make it all night) camping in the woods by Lums Pond. We'll take the ferry to visit Fort Delaware, then cross a haunted bridge on our way to see the ghosts haunting Dover, Delaware's capital. Then we'll spend some time with the witches of Lewes and Bridgeville and Millsboro before crossing another haunted bridge (if we dare) and saying hello to the spirits guarding Old Christ Church in Laurel. Next, we're off to the coast to see the ghosts who haunt Bethany Beach before wrapping up our journey in the southern end of the state, where a monster waits for us in the Great Cypress Swamp.

It'll be a fun trip, full of surprises and suspense and of course a lot of local history. After all, what better way is there to learn about a place than by getting to know its ghosts?

Are you ready? Let's go!

Rockwood Mansion

Reviving the Past at Rockwood Mansion

In the town of Wilmington in northern Delaware sits Rockwood Mansion and Park. One look at this vast Victorian estate and you'll understand why ghosts would choose to stay there.

Rockwood Mansion shares its two hundred acres with several other buildings. There are gazebos, a gardener's cottage, and a carriage house that was once used to store horse-drawn carriages. But the most beautiful—and haunted—structure is the fifty-room mansion. Rockwood was built in the 1850s in the rural Gothic style, which accounts for the house's pointed arches and steeply pitched roof. Its many windows and redbrick chimneys give it a striking appearance, but it's the spirits inside that really make this Victorian home unique.

Rockwood was built by Joseph Shipley, who was born in Wilmington in 1795 but spent much of his adult life in Liverpool, England. There he made a fortune as a banker and fell in love with the Gothic style. Later in life, when his health began to decline, Shipley returned to Wilmington and started construction on Rockwood. The estate was designed by George Williams, the same man who designed Shipley's home in England, and it was the first example of Gothic architecture in Delaware.

Joseph Shipley moved into Rockwood in 1854, along with his gardener, his housekeeper, and his two dogs, Toby and Branker. He lived at Rockwood for the rest of his life and died there on May 9, 1867, at the age of seventy-two. Shipley never married or had any children, so he left his home to his sisters in his will. When his last surviving sister passed away in 1891, his niece Sarah Shipley Bringhurst bought the estate and gave it to her son, Edward Bringhurst, Jr. Edward and his wife Anna had four children: Bessie, Mary, Edith, and Edward III (who changed his name to Edward V after meeting England's King George V when he was twenty-seven).

A big family was just what Rockwood needed. The Bringhurst parents and children and their large staff of butlers, cooks, gardeners, maids, and housekeepers filled the mansion with activity and joyous noise. Little Edward, the youngest Bringhurst, was eight years old when his family moved to Rockwood. Can you imagine growing up in a house that big? In addition to his spacious home, Edward's parents also turned an old stone building on the property into a playhouse for their son. What a lucky kid! The ruins of Edward's playhouse still exist at Rockwood Park today.

Everything must come to an end. The young family grew up, grew old, and eventually passed away. Four of them died at Rockwood Mansion. First, the father, Edward Jr., passed away in 1912 at age seventy-seven, then his wife Anna in 1923 at age eighty. The oldest daughter, Bessie, died at age sixty-nine in 1932. Finally, Mary Bringhurst, who lived to be one hundred years old, died at Rockwood in 1965.

Mary left Rockwood to her niece, Nancy Bringhurst Sellers Hargraves, making it clear that she wanted the property to be preserved. Nancy, the last of the Bringhursts, seemed to agree: When she died in 1972, she left her family's historic home to a nonprofit organization. In 1976, Rockwood was added to the National Register of Historic Places and opened to the public as a museum, park, and event venue.

No living person called Rockwood home after 1972, but the mansion was far from empty. In addition to the many employees, volunteers, and guests who visit the property, it quickly became clear that some of the previous residents had *also* stuck around.

Apparently, the hauntings started when Nancy Hargraves was still living at Rockwood. Florence, a cook who worked for Mrs. Hargraves, had trouble sleeping in the house. She frequently woke to the sound of heavy breathing behind her, like someone gasping for breath.

The Bringhursts weren't the only people to live and die in the mansion. A gardener named John, who worked there when Mary was alive, also passed away in the house. He'd mowed the lawn on a hot day, then gone to his room in the servants' quarters to lie down. A short time later, his wife found him there, dead. Some of the staff believed it was the ghostly echoes of John's last breaths that haunted Florence.

Nancy Hargraves even experienced creepy sensations herself. One night when her husband was away and she was alone in the house, she kept hearing things walking around in the darkness outside her room. She got so scared she locked the bedroom door and barricaded it with chairs.

Now that Rockwood is open to the public, its spirits have become even more active. From strange noises to the eerie sensation that a presence is nearby to actual ghost sightings, the property has earned a reputation for being haunted and has been featured on *Ghost Hunters* and other shows about the paranormal. There are too many Rockwood ghost stories to share, but here are some of the creepiest and most bizarre encounters.

Multiple tour guides and visitors at the mansion have reported hearing the swishing of skirts on the servants' staircase. Hearing the sound of clothing rustling, they instinctively look up to see who is coming down the stairs, but no one is there.

A bathtub on the third floor has been known to fill itself. When the tub overflowed and caused damage, plumbers shut off the water to it. But *someone* really wanted their bath, because the tub filled *again*. Eventually, they had to remove the water pipes completely to prevent more damage to the room.

The door to Mary Bringhurst's bedroom also has a mind of its own. It often sticks so that it's almost impossible to open, even though the doorknob turns easily and there is no obvious reason why the door won't move. One tour guide at the mansion has found that if she asks nicely, the door will open for her. She speaks directly to Mary's ghost, telling her there are visitors who would like to see her lovely home. Then the door opens.

Some of the ghosts at Rockwood aren't human. The Bringhursts were big animal lovers. The family had over forty dogs through the years. When their beloved pets passed away, they buried them in a pet cemetery on the property. The grave markers are now gone, but it seems that some of the canine spirits remain.

Mary Bringhurst's Irish wolfhound is one of the

ghost dogs at Rockwood. In 2014, a guide named Alice was speaking to a group of guests when she felt a dog walk up next to her. She was already reaching down to pet it when she remembered that dogs weren't allowed at the museum. She looked down and saw a large shaggy black dog, just like the one that sat by Mary in a portrait that hung in the mansion. The apparition quickly disappeared, but its presence lingered. Another employee, who was allergic to dogs, walked in shortly afterward. She swore she could smell dog fur, and her allergies seemed to support her claim: When she came near the spot where Alice encountered the ghostly dog, her eyes began to water!

A photo taken at the mansion that same year showed a dog's face peering through the window . . . even though there were no dogs at the house. It's clear that the pets who lived at Rockwood are just as enthusiastic about sticking around as their owners. Who knows, maybe even Toby and Branker—old Joseph Shipley's dogs— are still wandering around somewhere.

Dogs aren't the only ghosts to appear in photos. Mary Bringhurst has also made an appearance in tourists' snapshots. There are two locations where Mary seems to make her presence known: her own bedroom on the second floor, and a butler's room on the first floor, where Mary slept in her final years, when it became too hard for her to use the stairs. Some say they have felt Mary reach out and touch them in these locations, and one guest actually fainted when they felt Mary's cold hand on their skin!

Most of the spirits who haunt Rockwood don't create much of a scare. They seem to just be minding their own business and enjoying spending the afterlife in their old home. But one ghost does cause a chill: the "Shadow Man." Visitors often report feeling uncomfortable near the old coal chutes in the mansion's basement, where the

Shadow Man is said to lurk. It's as though someone is watching them. Some have taken pictures of the place where they felt this creepy presence. When they look back at the photos, they see the figure of a man with dark, ghostly eyes.

Feeling skeptical about these paranormal encounters? So did Philip Nord, former director of the Rockwood Museum. He didn't believe in the spiritual sightings others described until he saw a ghost himself.

One night when Nord was closing up, he saw a man sitting in the tearoom. The man turned to look at him, and Nord felt chills envelop his whole body.

He said to the man, "I see you!" When he looked again, the apparition was gone. Nord believes he saw the ghost of Edward Bringhurst, Jr.

Whether you're hoping to see a ghost or looking to take a step back into the Victorian age, Rockwood Mansion and Park is a great place to spend a day. Just maybe stay away from the basement . . . .

Delaware's Own Headless Horseman

Have you heard the tale of the headless horseman? The spine-tingling story of the man who wanders the darkness searching for his head? The author Washington Irving made this terrifying figure famous in his story "The Legend of Sleepy Hollow." That tale, of course, was fiction. What many people don't realize is that Delaware has its own headless horseman, and this one is *real*.

In Newark, Delaware, on top of a small hill near South College Avenue and Interstate 95, stands a small rectangular church. Looking up the hill, you'll see the graveyard that surrounds it, with crooked tombstones dating back to the 1700s. You'll see the church's redbrick walls, old but relatively even . . . except for one spot. Between the two windows of the western wall, the bricks have been mended, altering the smooth pattern of the wall. This quaint little building is the Welsh Tract Old School Baptist Church, and that patch of repaired brick is where the story of Delaware's headless horseman begins.

In 1703, after having a falling out with their fellow Baptists in Philadelphia, the Welsh Baptists wanted a fresh start. They bought thirty thousand acres of land from William Penn, the founder of Pennsylvania, and moved their congregation to a piece of land that would one day be a part of Newark, Delaware. The church they built still stands today and was added to the National Register of Historic Places in 1973.

On September 3, 1777, the Welsh Tract Old School Baptist Church became witness to the only Revolutionary War battle fought on Delaware's soil: The Battle of Cooch's Bridge. The United States, led by Major General George Washington, fought against a battalion led by British Lieutenant General William Howe. The Americans were outnumbered in both soldiers and weaponry. The battle raged all day, from nine o'clock in the morning until after sunset, but the British army finally won.

Historians disagree about the number of people killed that fateful day, but we know that one of them was a young man named Charlie Miller. Eager to defend his country, Miller joined the American army as soon as he was old enough and impatiently awaited an opportunity to fight alongside his fellow countrymen. On September 3, 1777, he got his chance.

His last chance, as it turned out.

Charlie Miller died in the Battle of Cooch's Bridge when a cannonball took off his head before smashing into the western wall of the Welsh Tract Old School Baptist Church. The mended patch of bricks on the church wall marks the spot where the cannonball struck. Miller's white horse fled when its rider fell, and the young soldier's head was never found. It is thought that his body (or at least most of it) was buried alongside other soldiers in the church cemetery, though we don't know for sure.

It was a sudden and brutal death—it's no wonder that Charlie's spirit is not at rest! Over the years, multiple people have heard the sound of hoofbeats near the old Welsh church when no horses were around. Others have reported running into Charlie Miller's ghost. As they drive down the quiet road past the church with the mended brick wall, they see a white horse step out of the shadows carrying a headless rider. Lots of car crashes have been reported on this stretch of road. Could the frightening sight of Charlie Miller's ghost be the reason why?

So, if you're ever in Newark, Delaware, take a trip to see the Welsh Tract Old School Baptist Church and the spot where a cannonball left its mark on history. But stay alert—you just might see a headless horseman following you up the road from his unmarked grave.

Screams in the Night at Lums Pond State Park

Do you like hiking through nature? Or kayaking across a beautiful pond? How about ziplining through the treetops? Or camping under the stars? Now, let me ask you this... Would you enjoy hearing the disembodied screams of a woman murdered a hundred and fifty years ago?

If you answered yes to any of these questions, you should visit Lums Pond State Park near Bear, Delaware.

The park officially opened to the public in 1963, but the land's history goes back hundreds of years. The area was a popular hunting spot for Native American tribes long before Europeans arrived. In 1735, settlers created Lums Pond, the biggest freshwater pond in the state, by building a dam on St. Georges Creek. In the years leading up to the American Civil War, the woods around the pond were part of the Underground Railroad, the secret path used by enslaved men and women escaping to freedom in the North.

Lums Pond State Park is a lovely place to spend the day hiking, picnicking, fishing, or boating. However, when the sun goes down, the peaceful atmosphere of the park is often broken by the sights and sounds of the past.

Late at night, visitors hear noises like groups of people running quickly through the woods, even when no one is there. Sometimes they also catch sight of shadowy human shapes darting through the trees. Who are these phantom spirits sprinting through the park? The Underground Railroad was a dangerous journey. Not everyone survived their voyage to freedom. Could these be the ghosts of people still trying to flee from slavery? Or maybe the spirits date all the way back to the indigenous tribes who crept through the woods hunting for food? The events that led to these eerie encounters are guesses, but there's one ghost at Lums Ponds that is tied to a famous local legend.

In the 1870s, a Wilmington woman ran away from home. She had been badly mistreated there, and when she saw an opportunity to flee, she left in a hurry. She carried very few items, thinking only of safety, and she ran for miles, eventually arriving at Lums Pond. The trees around the pond would have been the perfect place to hide for the night . . . if she had not been followed. However, this poor runaway was not alone in the woods. Someone with wicked intentions was there, too.

The young woman tried to escape from her attacker, but she no longer had the energy to run.

She screamed and screamed for help as she tried to fight him off but, sadly, she lost her life on the banks of Lums Pond. Her body was found floating in the pond the next day. Her throat had been cut with a knife.

The murderer was never found. Some people believed a homeless man in the area who suffered from mental illness committed the horrible crime. Others speculated that her abusive family might have pursued her and killed her. Either way, the person who committed this evil act continued to walk free, while his victim went to her grave.

The name of the woman murdered at Lums Pond has been lost over time, but her story—and her screams—live on. For over a hundred years, the young runaway's screams have echoed across the darkness in the woods surrounding the pond. Campers at the state park wake in the moonlit hours to her piercing shrieks and cries for help. Some even pack up and leave in the middle of the night because the sounds of her screams are so horrible. On multiple occasions, the police have answered calls from park visitors reporting a woman screaming, but every time they investigate, their search turns up nothing.

No one heard the woeful woman's wails when she needed them to save her life. Now, in death, she won't let *anyone* forget her. She keeps screaming.

Restless Souls at Fort Delaware

Perhaps some night you'll find yourself taking the ferry across the Delaware River. As the sun sets, the sky darkens, and the wind picks up (bringing a bit of a chill to the back of your neck), you look across the water and see a light where no light should be. Yes, there is land over there, and a building, but it's closed this time of night, uninhabited by any living soul. You allow your eyes to adjust to the darkness until you see the light belongs to a lantern. You peer harder until you understand that the lantern is held by a man in a long black cloak. You squint a little more and gasp when you realize . . . he doesn't have a head.

You're looking at Fort Delaware, the most haunted place in the entire state.

In the middle of the Delaware River, just off the coast from Delaware City, sits Pea Patch Island. This tiny piece of land is only a mile long, but there are a *lot* of ghosts packed into that small space. When you know the history of the location, you'll understand why.

In 1773, military engineer Major Pierre L'Enfant proposed building a fort on Pea Patch Island, then known as Pip Ash Island. L'Enfant later became famous for designing the original layout of Washington D.C.

The fort faced delays from the start. In fact, construction didn't even begin until forty years after L'Enfant's proposal, and various problems kept it from being completed for another fifty years. First, the builders had to restructure the plans to account for flooding. Then many became sick with an unknown respiratory infection. Next, they realized the fort was cracking and sinking into the muddy ground. After that, the unfinished fort caught on fire.

The builders of the fort had to start all over. This time, they used stone and brick and were making good progress when a man named James Humphrey sued the U.S. government, saying he was the rightful owner of Pea Patch Island. Construction stopped for ten years while a legal battle over the property ensued. By the time the U.S. claimed victory, nature had reclaimed much of the unfinished fort, setting the government back even further. Construction began once again. Builders worked tirelessly six days a week, never leaving the island until finally in 1858, the pentagon-shaped, moat-enclosed structure was ready for use.

The construction of the fort encountered so many obstacles that some people thought it was cursed from the very beginning. Whether some outside force was trying to keep people from building on Pea Patch or not, the things Fort Delaware witnessed in the 1860s most certainly had a haunting effect on the little island. So haunting, in fact, that numerous paranormal investigators from various TV shows have visited the site in recent years, and they usually encounter something to thrill and terrify their viewers.

During the American Civil War, Fort Delaware saw no combat. However, the fort was used as a prison for Confederate soldiers, and the brutal conditions and inhumane treatment made the location as deadly as a battlefield.

One of the biggest problems on the island was disease. In addition to the mysterious respiratory infections the builders of the fort suffered, prisoners also died from pneumonia and illnesses they battled due to the terrible living conditions. The lack of insulation in the barracks made them stuffy and overheated in the summer and freezing cold in the winter, and the poor plumbing system meant that the moat around the prison was often full of human waste. Then a smallpox epidemic swept through the island, taking hundreds more lives with it.

Another cause of the misery at Fort Delaware was overcrowding. At one point, there were 12,595 Confederate prisoners on the island, which was meant to house no more than 4,000. The way the men were packed in so closely to each other made the diseases spread like wildfire. Those who were taken to the prison's hospital almost never returned.

On top of these issues, there was evidence of cruelty and mistreatment of the prisoners. Some were chained in the dungeons and fed only bread and water as punishment. These "dungeons" were actually casemates, thick-walled rooms beneath the fortress meant for storing weapons and gunpowder. They had only small windows, so very little light ever got to the prisoners here. Other prisoners were supposedly shot and killed at the fort, possibly for not following orders.

Conditions were so bad that some prisoners did unthinkable things to try to escape the island. Some tried to swim to the shore of Delaware's mainland. On July 15, 1862, nineteen people attempted this. None were captured, and some may have actually made it to safety, but it's certain that many drowned. A few prisoners were so desperate, they tried to escape through the island's faulty sewer system, a grisly way to try to make it to freedom. Most escape attempts were unsuccessful, which may be the reason why people traveling to Pea Patch Island sometimes see the ghostly images of human hands reaching for them out of the water.

One prisoner got away from Fort Delaware in a very unique and horrifying way. When officials realized they couldn't keep burying dead bodies on the small island, they started loading the corpses into simple wooden coffins and sending them to the mainland on the Death Boat to be buried in mass graves at Finn's Point. One man was so desperate to leave Fort Delaware he removed the dead body from a coffin and climbed in himself. He stayed inside, surrounded by other caskets full of corpses until they reached the cemetery at Finn's Point. Then he leaped from the coffin and escaped to safety. It's possible one of the cemetery workers that night went home with a very creepy story to tell his family.

In all, about 32,000 Confederate soldiers were imprisoned at Fort Delaware during the war, and 2,460 of them died there. Taken altogether with what we know of the circumstances of their imprisonment, this paints a bleak picture of life at Fort Delaware in the years between 1861 and 1865. It also explains why so many phantoms still haunt Pea Patch Island.

In 1951, Fort Delaware was declared a state park. Today, the fort is a tourist attraction, where guests are invited to visit the historic site, walk the trails of Pea Patch Island, and learn about the area's past from costumed guides who speak and act as if it were still the 1800s. The employees are so devoted to keeping history alive that they never break character. In order to get a tour guide to stop pretending it's 1864 and speak to you in a modern way, you must first ask them to "take off their hat." Only then will they answer your question as someone in the 21st century.

Employees and visitors alike have experienced eerie encounters at the fort. Cold spots appear in unlikely places, such as in the kitchen even when there's a fire in the stove. Disembodied voices float from behind the closed doors of rooms empty of any living person. Linda and Lee Jennings, a couple who work at Fort Delaware State Park, have both experienced strange things. In 2005, Linda was working in the kitchen when a woman in a dirty, singed apron suddenly appeared at her side. The woman wandered around, inspecting what the women were cooking on the stove. Then she turned and walked through a wall. Lee's otherworldly encounter was in the dungeons. He's heard hushed conversations and footsteps there and has had the distinct, unsettling feeling of being followed.

While many of the ghosts at Fort Delaware are anonymous specters of the past, some have names and identities. One of the phantoms who haunts the island is Private Stefano, a Union soldier whose job was guarding the high-ranking Confederate officers at the prison. The jailors worried that the officers might rally their imprisoned men to revolt. So, the officers were kept away from the rest of the soldiers, housed in rooms above the entrance to the fort, up a steep stone staircase. One day, on the way down from his post, Private Stefano slipped and fell down the stairs to his death. But some say he never stopped guarding his post. Visitors often feel like they're being watched as they enter the fort beneath the old officers' rooms. Some even see the apparition of a soldier walk past them before vanishing, or feel the touch of a ghostly hand on their elbow as they listen to the tour guide's speech. It's Private Stefano, still on the job after all these years.

A haunted building that used to be the site of a horrific prison may sound like a strange place to take children, but every year dozens of schools go on field trips to visit Fort Delaware State Park and learn the history behind this important location. Josh Hitchens, author of the book *Haunted History of Delaware*, was on a trip to the fort in the fifth grade when he came across something that wasn't on the tour.

Josh was walking through the dungeons where Confederate prisoners used to be chained in solitary confinement when he became separated from the rest of his class. Alone, frightened, and worried about getting in trouble for wandering away from the group, he was desperate to find his classmates. When he heard voices down a corridor, he followed the sound, hoping to find his teacher and friends. Instead, he realized the voices were coming from behind a closed cell door. He looked through the small, barred window and saw two men sitting at a table. One was dressed in a nice, clean Union uniform while the other had on the clothes of a Confederate soldier, but they were torn and dirty. The Union soldier looked at Josh, and he immediately felt like he was interrupting something he wasn't supposed to see. Maybe the two men were practicing for a scene on the tour or rehearsing a speech? Whatever the reason, Josh felt he should leave, so he made his way out of the dungeon and quickly reunited with his group. Luckily, the teacher had not realized he was missing.

Later, at the end of the tour, Josh politely asked the guide to "take off his hat." He told the man what he'd seen in the dungeon and asked what those employees were doing there. The color drained from the guide's face as he explained that no actors were stationed in the dungeon. Those cell doors were rusted shut and unable to be opened.

Young Josh Hitchens had just seen his first ghost.

Mournful Music at Fiddler's Bridge

Delaware's role in United States history is a complicated one. The state sided with the Union during the Civil War, choosing not to secede, or separate from the country, with the Confederacy. However, some Delaware residents owned slaves. The Underground Railroad, a network of people who helped guide slaves to freedom in the North, included stops in Delaware. On the other hand, the state was also known for capturing ex-slaves and selling them back to the South. The notorious Patty Cannon was the ringleader of this terrible opposite version of the Underground Railroad. She and her gang kidnapped, sold, and murdered countless people, including Black men and women who had been born free in the North.

In addition to its connections with slavery, Delaware was also the last state to abolish whipping as a form of legal punishment for a crime. These whippings were public, which meant people were invited to watch. In the first half of the 1900s, over 1,600 public whippings took place in Delaware. Most of the criminals who received this punishment were Black.

This information, while difficult to think about, is a part of Delaware's past and must be acknowledged along with the positive parts of the state. This darker side of Delaware comes into play in the sad story of Fiddler's Bridge.

In the early 1800s, a white man named Mr. Osborn had a farm on Scott Run River. Osborn owned two Black slaves, a man and a woman. The couple had a little boy named Jacob who they adored.

Jacob was a natural musician. From a very young age, he made music wherever and however he could. Eventually, he made himself a violin using a box, a tree branch, and string. With his makeshift instrument, little Jacob played his heart out. His parents loved his tunes, and they weren't the only ones. Jacob was so talented that people came from all around to hear him play.

One day, Jacob's family woke up to a wonderful surprise. Some kind person had left a real violin outside their door. No more homemade, tree-branch fiddle for Jacob. Now he had a real instrument! He played his new fiddle with his whole heart, and his music made other people's hearts sing, too.

But not everyone. Mr. Osborn hated the sound of Jacob's music, and he decided to put an end to it.

One night, Mr. Osborn whipped Jacob so viciously for playing his fiddle that the young boy ended up unconscious with a battered body and bleeding ears. When he awoke from his beating, the boy was confused and ill for days. Although he eventually recovered physically, Jacob never spoke again. He continued to play his violin, but the music had changed. The tunes that came from his bow were still beautiful, but now they were filled with the sadness of his spirit.

Jacob left the farm and went to live in the woods nearby. His tormenter did not stop him from leaving. Jacob settled under the bridge over Scott Run, and there he stayed, playing his fiddle. His parents brought him food each day and listened to him play. His music reached other ears, too. People crossing the bridge often stopped to hear Jacob's tunes. Sometimes they tossed a coin down to him. He'd nod in thanks, never speaking, and continue to play.

One night, just around midnight, the neighbors who lived near the bridge noticed how quiet it suddenly was. The music had stopped. The next morning, when Jacob's mother and father came to the bridge to bring him food, they found their son dead. He was face-down in the water, still holding tight to his beloved fiddle.

No one knows whether Jacob died as the result of an accident or if he was the victim of something more sinister. What we do know is that not even death could put an end to his music.

Jacob's parents buried him with his fiddle. It wasn't long after his funeral that strange things started happening at the bridge over Scott Run. A group of men was crossing the bridge at midnight when they decided to stop and pay their respects to Jacob. One of the men tossed a silver coin into the water beneath the bridge. Then, all of them felt the hairs stand up on their arms and the back of their necks as the haunting tune of a fiddle floated up out of the darkness. At that moment, the legend of Fiddler's Bridge was born: toss a coin into the water at midnight, and Jacob will begin to play from beyond the grave.

The bridge where Jacob lived was just south of the modern town of St. Georges. The actual bridge is long gone, and Dupont Parkway, a multilane highway otherwise known as U.S. Route 13, now stretches above the place where the young fiddler used to play. The main sound you'll hear at that location now is the rumble of traffic rolling by, but that doesn't mean Jacob's spirit is gone. If you ever find yourself on Route 13 at midnight, toss a coin into the water, and see what happens. If you listen very closely, you may still hear the sad song of a fiddle drifting through the night.

Bullies Beware

Unfortunately, the world is full of bullies, and most of us have had to deal with one at some point in our lives. However, cruelty and name-calling aren't exclusive to the 21st century. Bullies existed in the 1700s, too. One Delaware man dealt with his tormentors in a unique way. He got back at them from beyond the grave.

Dover became the capital of Delaware in 1777, and taking a trip to downtown Dover today feels like taking a step back in time. First State Heritage Park on Dover Green offers a glimpse of Delaware as it used to be—with well-preserved buildings such as the Old State House, the Kent County Courthouse, the Parke-Ridgely House, and the Golden Fleece Tavern looking much as they did two hundred fifty years ago. These buildings witnessed a lot of historic events in our country's early days. The Golden Fleece Tavern was where Delaware became the First State when delegates met there on December 7, 1787, to ratify, or approve, the U.S. Constitution.

In addition to being a historical and cultural site, Dover Green is also the setting of a ghost story.

Samuel Chew was born the day before Halloween in 1693. He lived in Maryland for the first forty years of his life, then moved to Kent County, Delaware, in 1738 after his wife passed away. In 1741, he was named chief justice of Delaware by John Penn, the governor of Pennsylvania. For the next two years, Chew served the court and presided over cases until he passed away on June 16, 1843, at the age of fifty.

Despite being an educated man with an important role in the community, Samuel Chew endured constant mocking over the most ridiculous thing: his name. Some insensitive people in Dover thought "Chew" was a funny last name, and they teased Samuel about it mercilessly. When the chief justice walked through Dover Green or sat on a bench outside the courthouse, his peers would shout, "Achoo!" in a loud, fake sneeze or make overly exaggerated chewing sounds. This occurred every time Samuel Chew appeared in public, even when he was dressed in his judge's black robe and white wig.

Chew did not respond to the disrespectful taunts and never acted like they bothered him, but no one likes to be picked on. No matter how easygoing or forgiving he appeared on the outside, this behavior must have had an effect on him. After all, his bullies were relentless. They even made sneezing and chewing noises at his funeral!

The chief justice may have tolerated his bullies when he was alive . . . but after he died, they were the ones that could not rest. Shortly after Chew was buried, his ghost began appearing on Dover Green. A man passing through the park one night saw a figure standing solemnly under the chief justice's favorite tree. As he drew closer, he realized it *was* the chief justice, in spirit form. A few nights later, another man known to make fun of Chew saw the ghost at the same place. Only, this time, the shadowy figure crooked a finger at the man, as if asking him to come nearer. (He did not.)

These creepy encounters continued for more than two years. People began to avoid Dover Green at night, because no one wanted to run into the phantom. They had no desire to be judged for their misconduct toward the chief justice, especially by his ghost. Finally, the bullies couldn't stand it any longer. They met at the Eagle Tavern one night and formed a plan.

The following day, the community members who used to mock Samuel Chew gathered together to give the man the respectful funeral he deserved.

They dug a grave beneath the tree on Dover Green where his ghost had been seen. Then six of Chew's bullies carried an empty coffin to the makeshift gravesite and gently lowered it into the earth. There, they buried the chief justice's spirit, and not one person sneezed or chomped their teeth or said a rude word about the man.

This symbolic apology seemed to work. The ghost stopped appearing . . . until recently. Over a hundred and fifty years after Chew's second funeral, visitors to the First State Heritage Park on Dover Green have reported seeing a phantom in a judge's robe wandering around after dark. Why has the chief justice returned? Maybe he just wants to spend a little time in a place that still looks and feels like home. Then again, maybe he's back to cast judgment on those who have done wrong.

Bullies beware: If you visit Dover Green after the sun goes down, you may find yourself face-to-face with a ghost who wants to have a chat with you.

Woodburn Mansion

A Gathering of Ghosts at Woodburn

Woodburn Mansion has been the official Governor's House since 1965. In 1985, when Michael Castle became the governor of Delaware, he became its newest resident. On the day of his inauguration, dozens of people gathered at Woodburn to see Castle's swearing-in ceremony and celebrate his success. It was a happy occasion . . . with an eerie twist. Several of the guests in attendance had the same ghostly experience: They would feel a tug on their clothing and look down, expecting to see a lost child looking for their parent. Only, that wouldn't make sense because there weren't any children at the ceremony. What made even less sense was the fact that when they looked down, no one was there.

A few people, however, *did* spot a child. While Castle was being sworn in as governor of Delaware, they glimpsed a little girl standing in the corner. She was wearing a red and white checkered dress and a bonnet, not exactly a trendy style for children in the 1980s. That's because she wasn't from their time. The little girl in the red gingham dress is one of the ghosts that haunts Woodburn.

Situated in Delaware's capital, just a short distance away from Dover Green where the ghost of Samuel Chew hangs out, the Woodburn mansion is another popular spot for spirits. Charles Hillyard III built the house in the late 1700s and raised his family there. Some claim he was a harsh parent, known to punish his children by making them stand on their toes for long periods of time and whipping their feet if they let their heels touch the ground. Others say this is an exaggeration. However, one door in Woodburn shows evidence of violence: a patch over the hole left by a bullet, fired inside the house. Sources disagree about who fired the bullet: Hillyard aiming at his son or the son attempting to shoot his father. Either way, it's clear there was definitely some conflict in the family home.

In addition to being Woodburn's original owner, Charles Hillyard III was also the first ghost to appear in the house. Hillyard's daughter Mary inherited the property after her father died in 1814. About a year later, she and her husband, Martin W. Bates, had a guest staying with them, a Methodist preacher named Lorenzo Dow. One morning, Dow passed a man on the stairs dressed in old-fashioned clothes. The two men nodded at each other but did not speak. Later, Dow asked the Bateses about the other guest. They stared at him in confusion, explaining that no other guests had arrived. When the preacher gave details about the man he'd seen, Mary Bates told him he'd just described her deceased father.

The next owner of the Woodburn house was Daniel Cowgill. Cowgill was an abolitionist, which means he opposed slavery and worked to put an end to it. He freed the people his family had kept enslaved and offered his home to Black men and women who needed a safe place to meet. He even built a secret tunnel from his basement to a nearby river to be used by slaves escaping to freedom via the Underground Railroad. (The tunnel has since been sealed up.)

While Daniel Cowgill was doing his best to help end slavery, other cruel-hearted people were trying to do the opposite. Patty Cannon was notorious for catching escaped slaves and selling them back into slavery. She even kidnapped Black men and women who were born free in the North and sold them to slave owners in the South. Patty and her gang learned that Cowgill was helping escaped slaves, and they formed a plan to break into the house and abduct the people sheltering there.

Fortunately, Cowgill knew the gang was coming. When they arrived at Woodburn around midnight with their malicious intentions, he fired a rifle in the air several times to scare them off. The threat worked, mostly. Everyone ran away except for one man. Undeterred, he climbed a poplar tree on the property, most likely intending to wait until the coast was clear and continue his mission. His plan was thwarted when he slipped and fell. If the man had hit the ground from the height of his climb, he might have survived. Instead, on the way down his neck became stuck between two tree branches. The slave hunter hung there, unable to free himself, choking and gasping for breath until he finally died sometime in the early morning.

If the inhabitants of Woodburn heard the would-be kidnapper's agony, they ignored it. The following day, they removed his lifeless corpse from the tree.

Though the man's body was gone, the sounds of his last hours remained. For years, when people walked past what became known as "The Hanging Tree" late at night, they heard the gruesome sounds of a man strangling to death. The tree was cut down in 1999, and the area has remained quiet ever since.

The ghostly sounds of the hanging man may be gone, but Charles Hillyard III's spirit is still around. Strange occurrences have been known to happen in Hillyard's old bedroom. Frank Hall, a dentist who bought Woodburn in 1918, eventually locked the room and wouldn't allow anyone to sleep in it after both he and guests experienced disturbing nights there. One guest screamed and fainted after opening the door and seeing Hillyard's ghost standing there. When Hall slept in the "Ghost Room," as he called it, noises and knocking repeatedly interrupted his slumber. In the morning, he found the glasses he kept on his bedside table smashed on the floor by the open door, which had been closed and locked when he went to bed.

Hillyard's phantom appears to have some anger issues, but there's one more ghost at

Woodburn that seems to be having a good time.

The first governor to move into Woodburn after it became the official governor's residence in 1965 was Charles L. Terry. His wife, Jessica Irby Terry, was the first person to encounter a spirit in the dining room. "The Tippling Ghost" was named for his habit of drinking alcohol. The ghost, who appears in the clothing of a Revolutionary War soldier, has been seen sitting in the dining room sipping a glass of wine. If wine glasses are left in the room overnight, their contents mysteriously disappear by morning. "The Tippling Ghost" doesn't cause anyone any trouble. He seems to just be looking for a quiet place to wind down and enjoy a beverage in his afterlife.

Tours of Woodburn Mansion are open to the public by appointment, so if you're in the area, make some time to visit this historic home. While you're there, keep an eye out for the original owner, the thirsty soldier, and the little girl in the checkered dress.

The Bad Weather Witch and Other Things That Lurk Around Lewes

If you're in Delaware around Halloween, you should grab your broomstick and head over to Rehoboth Beach for the annual Sea Witch Festival. This lively event has been entertaining people since 1989 with parades, costume competitions, hayrides, broom-tossing contests, art, games, and more. The Sea Witch Festival is named after a record-breaking ship captained by Robert Waterman. In 1849, the *Sea Witch* sailed from China to New York in only seventy-five days.

While families celebrate at the Sea Witch Festival with costumes and trick-or-treating, a few miles up the coast at Cape Henlopen, sailors are haunted by a witch of their own, the Bad Weather Witch.

In 1798, a ship in the British Royal Navy called the HMS *De Braak* was sailing near Lewes, Delaware. The captain of the *De Braak* was James Drew, a soldier who had made a name for himself in the Revolutionary War for his viciousness toward both the living and the dead. Drew once dug up the grave of a personal enemy just to spit on the man's corpse and cut off its head.

Captain Drew was proud to be in charge of the *De Braak*, which was carrying a substantial amount of treasure looted from Spanish ships. When dark clouds rolled in near Cape Henlopen, Drew ignored them. He wouldn't allow his crew to take in the sails. This was a fatal mistake. A brutal storm broke out, pummeling the ship with rain and wind, sinking the *De Braak*, its treasure, and its crew in mere minutes. Forty-seven soldiers died off the coast of Lewes that night, including Captain James Drew, whose body washed up on the shore.

For centuries, divers have searched for the lost treasure of the sunken ship, but no one has ever found it. In 1935, a man named Charles N. Colstad felt like he was close to discovery when a severe thunderstorm rumbled in out of nowhere and forced his team to cancel their mission. That's when they began to think the treasure was cursed and protected by an otherworldly force that prevented anyone from finding it. The crew called this entity the Bad Weather Witch, and they were determined to banish her.

First, the sailors drew a picture of the evil spirit

and riddled it with bullets. When that didn't chase the storms away, they made a dummy of a witch. It had a pointed hat, long gray hair, a flowing cape, and a broom. They placed this witch doll in the best seat of their ship's cabin and offered her gifts of food and drink. Then they stuffed the fake witch into the stove in the galley, a ship's kitchen, and burned it. Afterward, they scattered the ashes across the water.

Not only did Colstad's ritual fail, it seemed to anger the Bad Weather Witch even more. The storm grew even stronger, tossing the ship and making any more dives impossible. Finally, Colstad and his crew admitted defeat and gave up their search for the treasure of the *De Braak*.

In 1986, the *De Braak* was finally raised from the seabed. Many historical artifacts from the shipwreck were sent to the Zwaanendael Museum in Lewes to be put on display, but the location of the legendary treasure remains a mystery.

Some people claim you can still see the *De Braak* on stormy nights. The ghost ship floats passed Cape Henlopen manned by a crew of soggy skeletons before descending into the depths, while the skeletons scream as they return once again to their watery grave.

These aren't the only seafaring specters still making appearances in Lewes. Beneath the parking lot for the Cape May–Lewes Ferry are hundreds of anonymous sailors whose corpses washed ashore over the years. Their remains were buried in a mass grave which was later covered and paved to make the parking area. Some of them are not resting peacefully.

Ferry employees say the terminal is not somewhere you want to bc alonc. Doors open and close on their own. Hand dryers in the bathroom turn on by themselves. Items launch off shelves as if pushed by unseen hands. Sometimes the ghosts reveal themselves in more obvious ways. Multiple night shift workers have seen shadowy figures, and one woman even felt the touch of a cold, wet hand on her shoulder. If you're thinking maybe she just imagined it, then why did it leave a damp handprint on her shirt?

As if a Bad Weather Witch and phantom sailors aren't enough, Lewes has even more supernatural activity to offer.

Two famous houses in Lewes have something very strange in common: they are both haunted by women named Susan who died tragic deaths. The Cannonball House on Front Street is now the location of the Lewes Historical Society, but it used to be the home of Susan Rowland King. King died on March 20, 1917, when an accidental fire broke out in her home. Ever since, the sound of ghostly footsteps haunts the house, and several people have reported feeling uncomfortable there. The door to King's bedroom also causes trouble. One owner of the house actually nailed the door shut because it would not stop opening. He left the house for a few days, and when he returned, the door was open again. The nails he had used were in a neat little pile on the floor.

The Ryves Holt House on Second Street is the oldest house in Delaware, and it also has a ghost named Susan. Susan Johnson died there in 1683 when she toppled down the house's staircase. Johnson's husband was accused of murdering her, but after all the evidence had been submitted, the jury cleared him, declaring her death an accident. However, odd occurrences in the Ryves Holt House led ghost hunters to explore it. In 2010, over three hundred and twenty years after Johnson died, paranormal investigators visited her former home. They brought a ghost box, which is a listening device used for capturing voices from the other side. The only word the device picked up was "pushed."

Maybe Susan Johnson's husband wasn't so innocent after all.

What about the mysterious monster that haunts campers with its screeches and wails and the beating of its large leathery wings? The creature that leaves large, strange footprints around tents during the night? This beast is known as the Henlopen Devil. Some say it's the offspring of the

famous Jersey Devil, a goat-headed, bat-winged, forked-tailed, hooved creature that haunts the Pine Barrens one hundred and fifty miles north of Lewes in New Jersey. Whatever it is, it's known to give campers in Cape Henlopen State Park a fright.

From supernatural weather phenomena to vengeful ghosts and forest devils, it's clear that Lewes is a location that fans of the paranormal won't want to miss.

Witches in the Woods

By now you know that if you visit Delaware, you'd better keep your eye out for ghosts. But the dead aren't the only creepy characters you need to watch out for. The state has also had its share of witches.

One witch who made a name for herself near Bridgeville many years ago was a woman named Dill Robinson. Robinson was skilled in her craft and could create spells for both good and evil. Some people paid her to concoct remedies or charms, and sometimes she performed her magic for free . . . and for meanness. She could put a hex on a person that would make them lose their appetite and shrivel to nothing. Sometimes they were able to convince her, with a small payment, to remove the spell.

One man, however, could not persuade the witch to take away his suffering, so he took matters into his own hands. He drew a picture of Dill Robinson, loaded his gun with silver bullets (since regular lead ones would not work on witches) and shot the picture. At that exact moment, eight miles away, Robinson fell over dead in her carriage. But was the man relieved of his curse? That detail remains unknown.

Another famous Sussex County witch was "Old Moll." Her real name was Mollie Kehonk, and she lived alone in a cabin in the woods near Millsboro. The locals were frightened of Old Moll and used to warn their children never to play in the woods or, "Old Moll will get ya!" If a child did go missing in the area, rumors always circulated that the witch had taken them for her dark magic.

Old Moll's witchcraft extended beyond mere spells and curses. According to legend, she was a shape-shifter. It was this extraordinary supernatural power that led to her downfall. One day, some boys ignored their parents' warning about the woods and went fox hunting there. When the witch saw them and told them to leave, they ignored her, too. Soon, the boys caught sight of the largest fox they'd ever seen. The pursued it through the woods until finally they were close enough to take a shot. The cry they heard after they fired their gun sounded more human than animal. When the boys investigated their kill, they didn't find a dead fox. Instead, they found the body of Old Moll.

The question is, will the spirits of these murdered women ever decide to return to the land of the living? Because a ghost is bad enough, but the ghost of a witch . . . ? That sounds like a whole new level of terrifying!

The Haunting of Maggie's Bridge

In Seaford, Delaware, on an otherwise ordinary stretch of road near the Woodland Ferry is one of the state's most haunted locations. The story behind Maggie's Bridge is tragic and gruesome, and the sights and sounds people have witnessed there will chill you to the bone. Beware: this tale is not for the faint of heart.

In the late 1800s, on a rainy night, a young pregnant woman named Maggie Bloxom was driving a horse-drawn carriage down what today is known as Woodland Church Road. Around midnight, just as Maggie was crossing a bridge over a small creek, a flash of lightning and burst of thunder startled her horse. The creature reared up, sending the entire carriage off the bridge and into the creek bed below. The accident was so violent that it took Maggie's life and her baby and her head. When her body was found the next day, she had been decapitated.

It's no wonder that a death so shocking and sudden would produce a ghost. According to locals, even though Maggie's body is buried in a small family graveyard nearby, the poor girl's spirit has never left the bridge. For over a hundred years, people have visited the spot where Maggie died in an attempt to lure her ghost to appear. Sometimes they are successful. But once they see and hear Maggie's phantom, they often regret their choice.

For those eager to meet Maggie, the legend says the best time to go looking for her is after midnight. Bonus if it's a full moon. They are instructed to stand on the bridge, looking over the small guardrail that separates the road from the creek below, and call for her. "Maggie! Maggie!"

The first time they call her name, they might not see anything, but they should listen carefully, because Maggie often appears initially as a sound: the wailing sob of a woman or even the rumbling of a ghostly carriage coming down the road. If the visitor's courage is still with them after that, they might try again. "Maggie! Maggie!"

The second time they call, the hairs will likely stand up on the back of their neck as they see a shadowy shape moving through the darkness. Maybe strange lights appear here and there. Not fireflies, no, these are otherworldly orbs floating through the trees around the creek. The sound of a mourning woman may intensify, and with it, they might hear the cries of a newborn baby.

Most people have left the bridge by this point. They've gotten back into their cars, started the engine with shaking fingers and sped off into the night toward home, toward life, toward safety. But if somehow, the visitor is still on that bridge, if they've convinced their feet to stay where they are despite all their instincts telling them to run, they might call for the ghost yet again. People say the best way to make her appear is to say, "Maggie, I have your baby!"

Now they've got her attention.

The shadow in the trees forms into a shape. The shape is human, a woman. It is the shape of a woman without a head. As she slowly makes her way toward the visitor on the bridge, they see that she is carrying something. It's her own severed head.

Now is the time to leave. It's probably important to mention that visitors should always make sure their car is full of gas before they make a stop at Maggie's Bridge.

A quick note from the author: Personally, I find the details of Maggie's haunting to be a bit cruel. Taunting ghosts is never a good idea, in my opinion, especially when they've lost as much as poor Maggie. I've done a little ghost-taunting in my life, including throwing rocks at the haunted shed in my childhood backyard, but I regret harassing that ghost. He didn't deserve to be annoyed by a bored kid, and neither does Maggie. Maybe it's time to let her rest in peace.

Perhaps I'm overly sensitive to this story for personal reasons. A year ago, I rescued and adopted a stray kitten who has brought much joy and laughter to my life. His mother still lives on our property. She's too wild to let inside, but I feed her, and she tolerates me even though I stole her baby. Her name is Maggie.

So, if you decide to visit the little bridge on Woodland Church Road at midnight, consider sending some kindness to the spirit of Maggie Bloxom. Instead of telling her you have her baby, perhaps you should call out, "Maggie, everything is okay! You and your child can rest easy now." Who knows how she might thank you?

Old Christ Church

Safeguarding Spirits at Old Christ Church

Many ghosts—most of them in fact—pose no harm to the living. Some even seem protective of the places they haunt, watching over the people who come and go. This is true of the spirits who reside at Old Christ Church near Chipman's Pond in Laurel.

Old Christ Church, also known as Old Lightwood, is a special place. It was built in 1772 when that area of Delaware was still part of

Maryland, and very little about the structure has altered since. The exterior of the wood-paneled walls and barrel-vaulted ceiling have been restored to keep them in good condition, but they look just as they did one hundred and fifty years ago. The inside has undergone even less change. The church has never added electricity or indoor plumbing, and the forty-three boxed pews and upper gallery are the same ones that parishioners used in the 18th century. The thirteenth pew even has a hex sign someone carved into it long ago, no doubt to ward off any effects of the unlucky number.

These aspects of the building, which was added to the National Register of Historic Places in 1972, make it unique, but it's the people who love the church that make it special. The Old Christ Church League is a non-profit organization dedicated to caring for and preserving the treasured structure. In addition to holding special services at the church, the League also opens it for tours. Each time Old Christ Church welcomes the public in, they open the shutters and prop the doors wide to let in the sunlight and fresh air. Stepping inside is like crossing the threshold of history, and guests are immediately met with the woody aroma of the building's original boards.

Behind the church is a cemetery, its tombstones dating back to the building's early days. One famous resident of the Old Christ Cemetery is Nathaniel Mitchell. He was a soldier in the Revolutionary War and a member of the Continental Congress, and from 1805 to 1808 he served as the governor of Delaware. The graveyard looks small, but that's only because so many of the graves are unmarked.

Don't be fooled: many corpses rest beneath your feet when you walk through there. Perhaps it's some of these folks who still show up from time to time at church services.

One of the ghosts at Old Christ Church is a woman in a long black dress wearing a bonnet or veil. She's been glimpsed standing in the doorway of the church during services, but whenever anyone tries to approach her, she steps out the door and immediately disappears. The other apparition was caught on camera. In the photo, it appears as a blurred white light that is roughly shaped like a person. The people who witnessed it

firsthand said the light inexplicably gathered into the shape and just as quickly dispersed again. One woman thought the shape looked like a little girl wearing a bonnet.

Whoever these spirits are, it's obvious they mean no harm to the worshippers of Old Christ Church. They, like the Old Christ Church League, just seem to be keeping watch over an old building that means a lot to the state of Delaware.

CH. / PED. 8
CH. / PED. 4
POS. / PED. 8
POS. / PED. 4
ANTIPHONAL
2
3
4
POS./PED.
1
2
GENERAL
1
2
3
4
5
6
GENERAL
7
8
9
10
11
12

A Splash of Spookiness at Bethany Beach

Bethany Beach, on the southern end of Delaware's coast, offers visitors a calmer, quieter stay than some of the state's other seaside locations. The town's beautiful beaches and charming cottages radiate serenity and relaxation. However, there is one historic inn on Bethany Beach that gives its guests a little something extra: ghosts.

The Addy Sea was built as a private home in 1901. John and Jennie Addy, a couple from

Pittsburgh, Pennsylvania, wanted a summer house on the beach to enjoy with their four children. John was a plumber, so he was able to do some of the work on the house himself. The luxurious home was the first on Bethany Beach to have indoor plumbing and gas lighting indoors.

The address of the Addy Sea is on Ocean View Parkway, but that is not its original location. The house was moved twice after vicious storms in 1920 and 1927 almost destroyed it. Still the Addy Sea persevered and has now been at its current site for almost one hundred years. In 1935, while struggling with finances during the Great Depression, the Addy family first began renting rooms to tourists. In 1974, they sold the Addy Sea to Leroy and Frances Gravatte, who continued to use the historic structure as a bed and breakfast. As of the writing of this book, the Gravatte family still owns and manages the Addy Sea.

The house is beautiful inside and out. Victorian era décor, marble fireplaces, tin ceilings, and elegant antique furniture all give this bed and breakfast the feeling of being transported back in time. However, modern comforts such as air conditioners and one television ensure visitors don't feel *too* far away from the 21st century. The Addy Sea is right on the beach, so it's just as easy to enjoy the beautiful ocean views from a rocking chair on the spacious porch as it is to venture along the shore looking for seashells.

In addition to serenity and comfort and gorgeous views, people also come to the Addy Sea for the ghosts.

It's important to note that the bed and breakfast's current manager does not believe the inn is haunted. She has never experienced any ghostly phenomena herself. Nevertheless, multiple people over the years have witnessed strange occurrences, including Frances Gravatte.

When the Gravattes first purchased the Addy Sea, Frances was alone in the house cleaning out a closet when the door suddenly closed and locked behind her. When a busboy came in from outside and heard her banging on the closet door, he rescued her. Neither of them could figure out who, or what, had locked her in.

Guests in rooms 1, 6, and 11 have also had their share of frights at the Addy Sea. Room 1 used to be the bedroom of John Addy, the house's original owner. John had a copper bathtub that he loved so much, he moved it all the way to Bethany Beach from Pittsburgh. Back when the copper tub was still in the Addy Sea, guests taking a bath in it would sometimes feel the tub begin to shake as if someone was rocking it back and forth. Perhaps John wanted these strangers out of his tub! In room 6, it was not a physical sensation that surprised visitors, but an auditory one. Guests sometimes hear the sound of organ music when staying in that room.

The most frequent hauntings, though, happen in room 11, which makes sense when you learn that the room has at least two ghosts: Kurtz Addy and Paul Delaney.

Kurtz Addy was a relative of the Addy family who was known for his moody and unpredictable behavior. Late one night in the 1920s when Kurtz was staying at the house, he plummeted off the roof to his death. Whether he fell or jumped is unknown, but ever since, guests in room 11 have heard heavy footsteps walking across the roof above them during the night.

Unlike Kurtz, Paul Delaney did not die at Bethany Beach. He worked as a repairman at the Addy Sea for many years, and owner Frances Gravatte believes his spirit returned there after his death. She has seen an apparition lying on the bed in room 11, and her granddaughter once felt the cold touch of an unseen hand there.

Guests have reported things that may be linked to Delaney's presence as well. One person wrote in their review of their stay at the Addy Sea that the jacuzzi shower kept turning on and off on its own. When they tried to record the odd behavior, their phone died. In the summer of 2020, Josh Hitchens (the same Josh Hitchens who saw his first ghost at Fort Delaware in the fifth grade) stayed in room 11 with his partner. Hitchens unplugged the bathroom nightlight before going to sleep. In the middle of the night, he awoke to a soft glow coming from the restroom. The seashell-shaped nightlight was back in the outlet, even though neither Hitchens nor his partner had put it there.

These eerie experiences could've been caused by the Addy Sea's old repairman. Maybe Paul

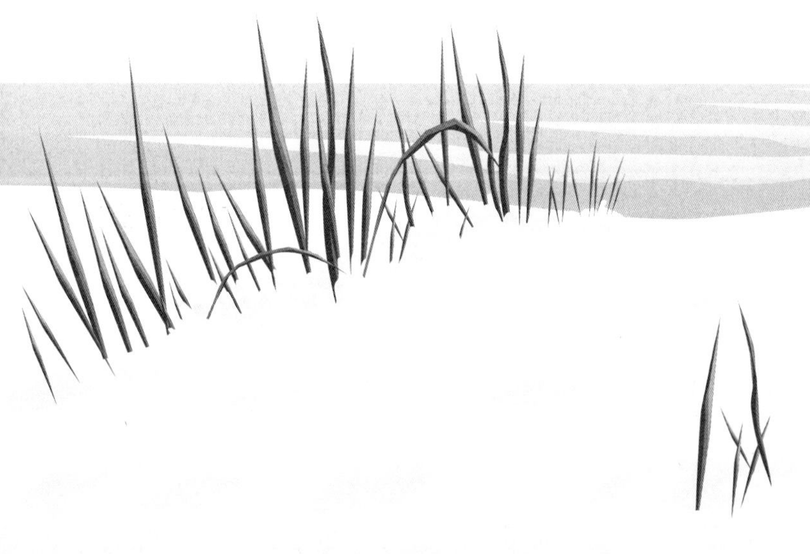

Delaney is just checking the showers and replacing the nightlights, trying to make sure the guests have a pleasant stay.

The Addy Sea is a unique bed and breakfast with a lot to offer those looking for an ocean getaway. Whether you see a ghost or not, a visit to this historic inn on Bethany Beach is worth the trip.

The Swamp Monster of Sussex County

A cryptid is a creature whose existence is questionable. There are stories of sightings and claims of encounters with these beasts, but no hard scientific facts to back them up. Dozens of cryptids have become famous in various parts of the world over the years. Bigfoot is on this list, as well as the Loch Ness Monster in Scotland, Champ in Lake Champlain in Vermont, and the Henlopen Devil, mentioned in a previous chapter. But Delaware has yet another famous cryptid on the southern border of the state: the Swamp Monster of Sussex County.

The Great Cypress Swamp, which has had many names over the years including the Great Pocomoke Swamp and the Burnt Swamp, is the largest freshwater swamp on the Delmarva Peninsula. Today, the swamp covers fifty square miles. It used to be larger before a devastating fire ravaged much of it in 1930. The fire burned for eight months, destroying thousands of acres of vegetation and killing most of the towering bald cypress trees that grew there. However, the swampland proved resilient. With the help of a non-profit organization called the Delaware Wild Lands, which has made it their mission to replant bald cypress trees, the swamp has healed itself from the terrible fire and remains an important natural area, home to dozens of species of birds.

Even when there's no monster present, this misty marshland can be spooky. The sunlight filtering through what's left of the towering cypress trees casts strange shadows, and the hanging moss can sometimes feel like it's reaching for you. But when you visit the swamp and suddenly realize you're not alone, things get even creepier.

For almost a hundred years, reports have circulated of a creature that haunts the Great Cypress Swamp. Shortly after the fire changed the swamp's landscape, two men went hunting there with their dogs. While walking through the trees looking for game, the dogs suddenly tucked their tails between their legs and started shaking in fear. The men were confused until they heard screams. Then they realized something was following them. The sound of snapping branches shadowed their footsteps as they made their way out of the swamp. They never saw the thing that screamed or the beast that chased them. When they made it back to safety, they wasted no time in leaving the area.

When teenagers in the 1960s claimed to see a hairy, moaning creature while driving through the swamp, most people brushed it off. Then adults started seeing it too—something covered in fur that looked like half man, half beast, or maybe a large animal standing on two legs.

Who or what is Delaware's swamp monster? Part of the mystery was solved in 2015 when a man from Selbyville named Fred Stevens came clean in an article for WHYY. His confession? *He* was the swamp monster . . . for a while at least.

In 1964, when Fred Stevens was twenty-one years old and rumors were spreading about a creature in the swamp near his home, he decided to have a little fun. Wearing a raccoon fur coat and various other monster-like attire, and carrying a baseball bat with spikes sticking out of it, Stevens would venture into the swamp at night, hide on the edge of the road, and jump out at people as they drove by. His friend, Ralph Grapperhaus, who worked for a local newspaper, published stories about these sightings, making Stevens's fake creature quite a celebrity. People started traveling from farther and farther away to try to get a glimpse of the Sussex County swamp monster. Stevens said some even brought gifts of food, such as chickens, to feed the beast.

Eventually, Stevens had to stop playing his little game. It was too dangerous. He was worried someone would shoot him in an attempt to kill the creature. So he hung up his raccoon skin coat and kept his secret for fifty years.

Stevens may have been the monster in 1964, but his antics don't explain the sightings before that or after. In 2004, a college student named John was driving through the Great Cypress Swamp when he encountered a figure standing seven or eight feet tall covered in thick black hair. When the creature casually turned its head and made eye contact with him, John's own hair stood up all over his body. He pressed the gas pedal to the floor and sped away without looking back.

Whatever John saw that night, it wasn't Fred Stevens.

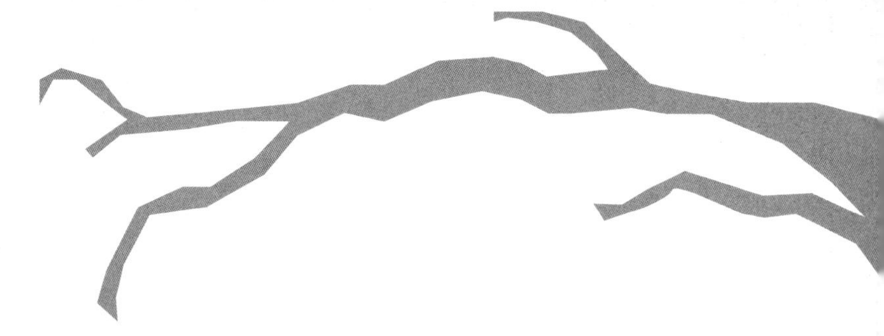

Safe Travels

Well? What are you waiting for? Grab a map, jump in the car, and take your own tour of the spooky sites in Delaware. But make sure your tank is full of gas, and don't forget to pack a flashlight, maybe some good running shoes, and definitely your courage. Because Delaware's roads, bridges, churches, houses, and woods are *full* of ghosts . . . and they're all eager to meet you.

Carie Juettner was born on Halloween and has loved ghost stories ever since. She is the author of five books in the *Spooky America* series. Carie lives in Richardson, Texas, with her husband and pets. When she's not writing, she enjoys reading, doing yoga, and taking long walks in the woods. To find out more about her books and what she's writing next, visit her website: cariejuettner.com.

Check out some of the other *Spooky America* titles available now!

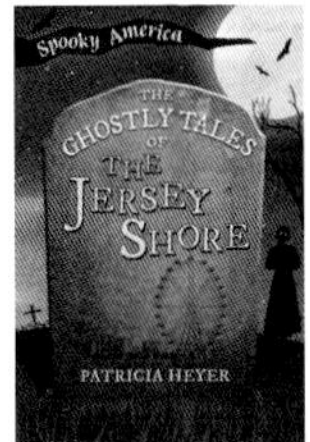

Spooky America was adapted from the creeptastic *Haunted America* series for adults. *Haunted America* explores historical haunts in cities and regions across America. Here's more from the original *Haunted History of Delaware* author, Josh Hitchens:

www.joshhitchens.com